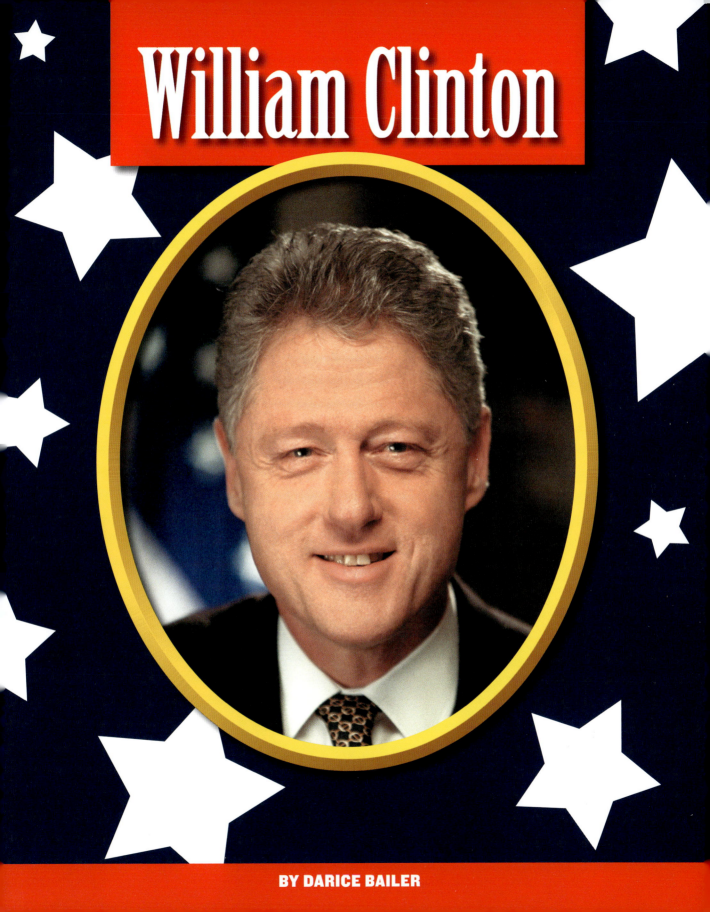

Published by The Child's World®
1980 Lookout Drive • Mankato, MN 56003-1705
800-599-READ • www.childsworld.com

Acknowledgments
The Child's World®: Mary Swensen, Publishing Director
Red Line Editorial: Editorial direction and production
The Design Lab: Design

Photographs ©: William J. Clinton Presidential Library, cover, 1, 4, 8, 15; Arnie Sachs/CNP/Corbis, 6; Warren K. Leffler/U.S. News & World Report Magazine Photograph Collection/Library of Congress, 10; Carl D. Walsh/Aurora Photos/Corbis, 13; Bettmann/Corbis, 16; Ed Reinke/AP Images, 19; Bebeto Matthews/AP Images, 21

Copyright © 2017 by The Child's World®
All rights reserved. No part of this book may be reproduced or utilized in any form or by any means without written permission from the publisher.

ISBN 9781503808805
LCCN 2015958438

Printed in the United States of America
Mankato, MN
June, 2016
PA02303

ABOUT THE AUTHOR

Darice Bailer is the author of many books for young readers, including biographies for The World's Greatest Artists series for The Child's World®, which were 2014 Junior Library Guild Selections for the Series Nonfiction Level: Social Studies. Her book *Measuring Temperature* was also a 2014 Junior Library Guild Selection for science. She lives in Connecticut with her family.

Table of Contents

CHAPTER ONE
On the Road to the White House. 5

CHAPTER TWO
Bill Grows Up 7

CHAPTER THREE
Off to Washington, DC. 11

CHAPTER FOUR
From Governor to President 17

Timeline 22
Glossary 23
To Learn More. 24
Index 24

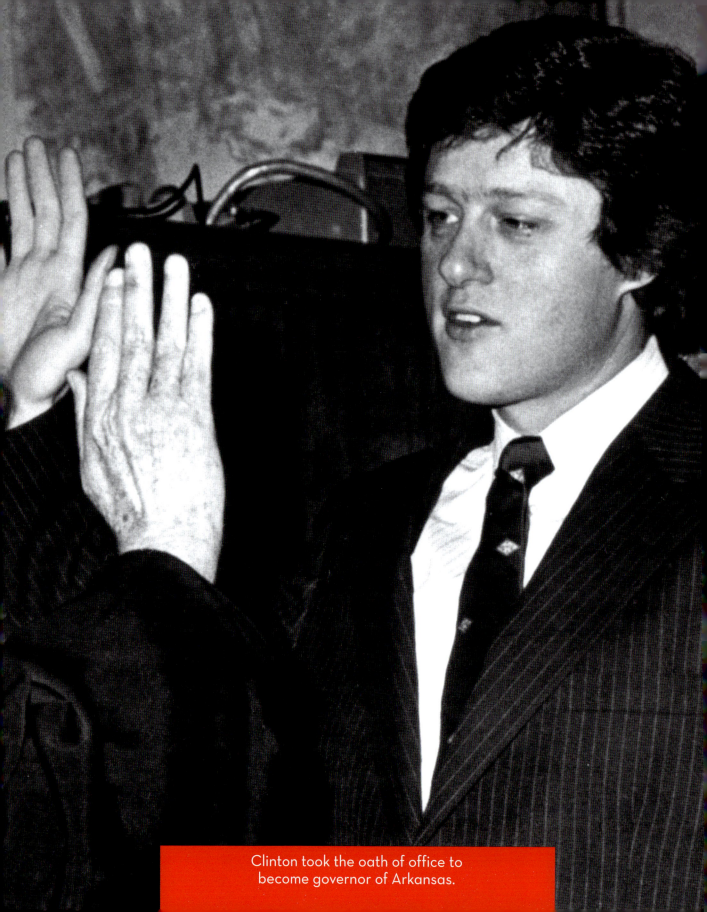
Clinton took the oath of office to become governor of Arkansas.

CHAPTER ONE

On the Road to the White House

Cameras flashed. It was January 9, 1979. William Jefferson Clinton raised his right hand. He took the **oath** of office as **governor** of Arkansas. William went by Bill. He was 32 years old. He was the youngest governor in the United States at that time.

Clinton spoke at his **inauguration**. Arkansas had many poor people. He wanted to make life easier for the poor and the **elderly**. He thought teachers should be paid more. He wanted to make schools better.

President Kennedy shook Clinton's hand on the White House lawn.

Clinton hoped to be a great governor. Some governors later become president. In high school, Clinton had dreamed of being president. When he was 16, he went on a trip to Washington, DC. He stood on the White House lawn. President John F. Kennedy shook his hand. Clinton went home and dreamed. His mother often told him he could be president. Now that he was governor, he was closer to that dream.

CHAPTER TWO

Bill Grows Up

Bill was born on August 19, 1946, in a town called Hope, Arkansas. His dad died in a car accident before Bill was born.

Bill lived with his mother and grandparents. Bill's grandparents helped raise him. Bill called them Mammaw and Papaw. Mammaw taught Bill numbers. She read to him every day. He could already read a little at three years old.

Bill's grandpa taught him to be kind to everyone. Papaw ran a small grocery store. In the 1940s, many white people were **racist**. They treated African

Bill grew up in Arkansas.

Americans unfairly. Some white people thought they were better than African Americans. Many African

8

Americans had trouble finding work. Some companies would not hire them. If they found a job, they were often paid less than white workers. This was not against the law. Papaw was different. Sometimes African Americans did not have money for food at his store. Papaw said they could pay later.

Bill was three when his mother remarried. Bill's new dad was Roger Clinton. The three of them moved to a big farm. But they did not have much money. The house did not have a bathroom. The family used a wooden outhouse in the yard.

As he grew up, Bill did well in school. He got mostly *A*s. But he talked too much in class. His sixth-grade teacher said he would either be a troublemaker or a governor.

In high school, Bill ran for class president. He won. He graduated near the top of his class.

In the early and mid-1900s, some businesses, including cabs, only served white people.

CHAPTER THREE

Off to Washington, DC

Bill Clinton watched Dr. Martin Luther King Jr. on television. It was August 28, 1963. King spoke to a big crowd in Washington, DC. He said that African Americans were treated unfairly. They were separated from white people. Signs kept African Americans out of restaurants and hotels. The signs read "For Whites Only." The U.S. Constitution said all men were created equal. But African Americans and white people were not treated like equals. Clinton wanted to change that.

After high school, Clinton decided to go to Washington, DC. That was where laws were made. He wanted to go into **politics**. He could make life better for everyone. Clinton applied to one college. It was Georgetown University in Washington, DC.

Clinton started school at Georgetown in September 1964. He ran for class president. Students liked his good looks and energy. He worked hard to get votes. He won the **election** two years in a row.

In 1970, Clinton started at Yale Law School. It was one of the best law schools in the country. He met a woman in the law library. Her name was Hillary Rodham. Clinton thought Hillary was the smartest woman he had ever met.

Clinton graduated in 1973. He taught law in Arkansas. Hillary joined him there. Then, he decided to start his career in politics. He ran for U.S. Senate.

Clinton attended Yale Law School where he met his wife, Hillary.

Clinton met as many voters as he could during his **campaign**. He would tell his driver to stop the car. Then, he would jump out to shake one person's hand. He thought if voters met him, they would like him.

Clinton lost the 1974 election. But Arkansans were impressed. And Clinton did not lose his political goals.

Meanwhile, Clinton married Hillary in 1975. Three years later, he became governor of Arkansas. He had his work cut out for him.

Clinton and Hillary married on October 11, 1975.

Clinton worked to improve Arkansas schools while he was governor.

CHAPTER FOUR

From Governor to President

The governor's mansion was a big house in Little Rock, Arkansas. In the fifth grade, Clinton's class visited the mansion. He sat down in the governor's chair. Now, it was his chair.

Clinton was governor of Arkansas for almost 12 years. He worked hard to fix schools. Every state spent more money on schools than Arkansas did. But under Clinton, the state raised its sales **tax**. Sales tax is money that people pay the government when they buy products. That money helped schools. Teachers were paid more.

While he was governor, Clinton also became a father. His daughter, Chelsea, was born in 1980. Eleven years later, Clinton decided to run for president. He had loved being governor. He had helped people in Arkansas. But now he wanted to help the whole country.

Some voters told Clinton sad stories. One woman said she did not have enough money to buy both food and medicine. Some parents had trouble finding jobs. They could not pay their bills. Clinton cared about these people. He hoped he could help.

In November 1992, Clinton won the election. His mother always said he would be president. Now, he was. "I loved seeing my mother's tears of joy, and I

Clinton took the oath of office as president on January 20, 1993.

hoped that my father was looking down on me with pride," he remembered.

The first law Clinton signed helped families. Some Americans could lose their jobs if they stayed home with a new baby. The new law gave most people three months off work when they have a baby.

They could also take three months off work to care for a sick family member.

Clinton served his first term. That is four years. Then, he was elected for a second term. During his second term, Congress thought he told a lie about someone who worked in the White House. They thought the lie hid evidence in the case against him. The House of Representatives voted to **impeach** Clinton. But the Senate found him not guilty a year later.

The country did well while Clinton was president. Companies made more products. They hired more workers. When Clinton left office, more than half of Americans thought he had done a good job. After leaving the White House, Clinton kept working. He raised money to end poverty and to help people be healthy. He also wrote books. One was an

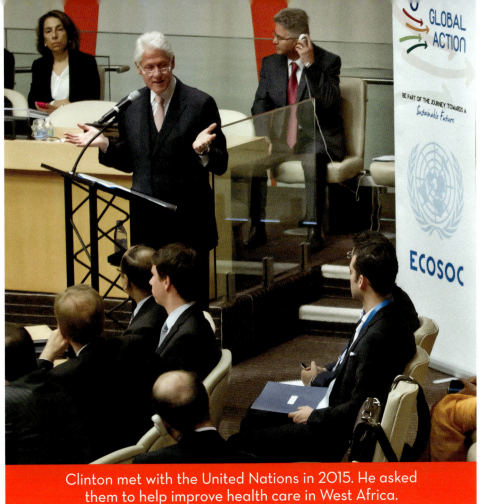

Clinton met with the United Nations in 2015. He asked them to help improve health care in West Africa.

autobiography called *My Life*. Clinton helped his wife, Hillary, run for office, too. She became senator of New York. He also helped her with her presidential campaigns.

Bill Clinton was a poor boy who dreamed of serving his country. He became president. His work has helped people around the world.

TIMELINE

←— **August 19, 1946** William Jefferson Clinton is born.

←— **July 24, 1963** President Kennedy shakes Clinton's hand at the White House.

←— **June 1968** Clinton graduates from Georgetown University.

←— **Fall 1970** Clinton starts Yale Law School.

←— **November 5, 1974** Clinton loses the election to the U.S. House of Representatives.

←— **October 11, 1975** Clinton marries Hillary Rodham in Arkansas.

←— **November 7, 1978** Clinton is elected governor of Arkansas.

←— **February 27, 1980** Chelsea Clinton is born. Clinton loses the race for reelection later that year.

←— **November 2, 1982** Clinton runs for governor again and wins.

←— **November 3, 1992** Clinton is elected 42nd president of the United States.

←— **November 5, 1996** Voters reelect Clinton as president for a second term.

←— **December 19, 1998** Clinton is impeached for lying under oath. The Senate finds him not guilty a year later.

←— **January 20, 2001** Clinton leaves office after his second term.

GLOSSARY

campaign (kam-PAYN) When people try to win an election, they organize their activities in a campaign. Bill Clinton met many voters during his campaign for Congress.

elderly (EL-dur-lee) A person who is elderly is old. Bill Clinton often stopped to chat with elderly people in wheelchairs.

election (i-LEK-shun) An election is when people choose a leader by voting. Bill Clinton won the 1992 presidential election.

governor (GUV-uh-ner) A governor is the head of a state or colony. Bill Clinton was governor of Arkansas.

impeach (im-PEECH) To impeach someone in office is to charge him or her with wrongdoing. The House of Representatives votes to impeach a president.

inauguration (in-aw-gyuh-RAY-shuhn) An inauguration is a special ceremony where an official takes office. At his first presidential inauguration, Bill Clinton said everyone in America should have a chance to succeed.

oath (OHTH) An oath is a formal promise. Bill Clinton began his first term as president when he took the oath of office.

politics (POL-uh-tiks) Politics are activities to gain or hold onto power in government. Some people get into politics to help people.

racist (RAY-sist) Someone who is racist thinks they're better than people with another skin color. Many white people in the 1960s were racist.

tax (TAKS) A tax is the money that people and companies pay the government. Bill Clinton raised the Arkansas sales tax, and that money helped improve schools.

TO LEARN MORE

In the Library

Gregory, Josh. *Bill Clinton*. New York: Children's Press, 2014.

Krull, Kathleen. *Hillary Rodham Clinton: Dreams Taking Flight*. New York: Simon & Schuster Books for Young Readers, 2015.

Venezia, Mike. *Bill Clinton: Forty-Second President*. New York: Children's Press, 2008.

On the Web

Visit our Web site for links about William Clinton: **childsworld.com/links**

Note to Parents, Teachers, and Librarians: We routinely verify our Web links to make sure they are safe and active sites. So encourage your readers to check them out!

INDEX

African Americans, 7–9, 11
Arkansas, 5, 7, 12, 17, 18

campaign, 12, 14, 18, 21
Clinton, Hillary Rodham, 12, 14, 21
Clinton, Roger, 9
Congress, 20

education, 5, 9, 12, 17–18

Georgetown University, 12
governor, 5–6, 9, 14, 17–18

Kennedy, John F., 6
King, Dr. Martin Luther, Jr., 11

president, 6, 9, 12, 18–20

Washington, DC, 6, 11, 12
White House, 6, 20

Yale Law School, 12